Message to the Masses

Julia A. Royston

BK
ROYSTON
Publishing

BK Royston Publishing
P. O. Box 4321
Jeffersonville, IN 47131
502-802-5385
http://bkroystonpublishing.com
bkroystonpublishing@gmail.com

© Copyright – 2014

Cover Design: Bill Lacy

ISBN-13: 978-0692311455
ISBN-10: 0692311459

Printed in the United States of America

Dedication

I dedicate this to every person who has ever been told that you are local, no one will ever know about you and you will not succeed. Prove them wrong and go do it.

I pray that you get the courage to keep going, strength from God to keep growing and knowledge from the masters to keep knowing.

Acknowledgements

I thank my Lord and Savior Jesus Christ for giving me another opportunity to introduce more people to you. I thank you that you have entrusted this gift to me. Lord, let your Spirit move, guide and empower through this book to the people who will read it.

To my husband, Brian K. Royston, the love of my life for loving and cheering me on so much that I can be and do all that God has placed in me. I love you...

To my Mom, who is a greatest supporter and best friend. To my Dad, who is in heaven, that I know is proud of me and always encouraged me to go for it. Thanks to all of the rest of my family for their love and support.

A special thank you to Rev. and Mrs. Claude R. Royston for their love and support. Papa thank you for using your fine tooth comb to edit this book again.

I dedicate this book to every person in the world. No matter the product, service, ministry, gift, talent, organization, business, small or great, let something that is written in this book help you to move closer to your goal of success and moving your Message to the Masses.

Love, Julia A. Royston

Table of Contents

Introduction

I have so many people come to me and ask, "How do I get my message out there?" When I start talking strategy, time and budget, they usually walk away and determine that they can do it another way. But, repeatedly, I have had people return to me and say, "I thought I could do it on my own. Or others say, I don't want to do it, I need help."

That's what this book is all about. Have a Message but being will to do what it takes to get it to the Masses.

You can have a powerful message, awesome products and services, a process as smooth as silk and a team that rivals any in the NBA, but if no one knows about what you have to offer, your business will fail and be non-existent.

How will you get your message to the masses? What will it take? It will take everything you have and more.

Turn the pages of this book and find out the many ways to get your message to the masses. Also, obtain the workbook to put your pen to paper and develop a strategy in black and white to get your Message to the Masses.

Julia A. Royston

Purpose and Message

There is an intended use and purpose for everything that is created. When you purchase anything from the grocery store, warehouse, or discount store, there is an intended use for that thing that you are purchasing. Some people may misuse the item even though on the box, back of the package or on the instructional sheet inside the box, it tells you specifically what the purpose of that item is. Some ointments list that it is intended for external use and not to be ingested by mouth. The purpose has to be spelled out and specified.

In business, this is no different. Your purpose should be spelled out. Your purpose should be clear and easily understood by all. You could include your purpose in a statement by itself or it could be included in a mission or vision statement.

When someone contacts BK Royston Publishing, LLC, we are specific about the fact that we are a full service publishing company. We are not in business to sell food, manufacture widgets or paint houses. The purpose of this company is to create great literary works for people to enjoy. There may be additional products and services that accompany our literary works but the purpose of our existence is to create, publish and promote literary works as defined by the U. S. Copyright Office. Our potential and current clients know quality literary works, our customers buy quality literary works and our staff is experienced in producing quality literary works.

What is your purpose for existence? What is the purpose of your book, business, ministry, coaching, training, non-profit, organization or community? This should be the first thing that you determine before delivering any message of any kind to anyone.

Message of the Purpose

Once you determine the purpose then you must determine the message of that purpose. You know your purpose but what is the message related to that purpose? So, back to my initial analogy of the publishing company. The purpose of the company is for publishing books but my message of my purpose is that BK Royston Publishing will treat you and your books like royalty. Our message is that we produce quality books that will inform, entertain and enlighten. We also treat our authors well and deliver what we promise in a timely manner.

If you have ever watched a Charlie Brown episode then you will know that his teacher never said any words that you could actually understand. It was just rhythmic noise. Have you ever received a voicemail message and the person gave their name, the date, and then said, 'my phone number is 555-12...' but you missed the last two numbers? In both of these instances, a message was delivered but, the receiver didn't actually receive the message that was delivered. Charlie Brown's teacher's voice was making sounds but, no clear words were uttered. This example is a little extreme but, even though two people can be speaking the same language to each other, a clear message may not be received. The voicemail message is a typical example. A message was delivered but, not completely. Part of the voicemail message was cut off. The message may have started off sounding good and the customer or client may be ready to buy but, something is missing. In this case, how will your customer or client call you back to get the rest of the message and/or respond to your offer since they didn't get the full message? You may have lost a sale forever. No matter if your organization has been established a day, month or decade, the message that your organization is attempting to deliver to its customer or client base will determine if your organization will still exist in the next day or week.	Whether you have an organization, leadership retreat or staff meeting, take some time to determine what the message is that you are trying to deliver, think about it.	When people come in contact with your organization whether in-person or online, what do they believe you are trying to say about your company?	Now, the message that you are trying to convey and the one that people receive may or may not be the same message.	There are some organizational leaders who wonder why they can't seem to get new business, keep repeat business or sustain their business.	It might be because there is a difference between the message that is being delivered and the message that they want to deliver.	You need to take the time to make sure that you know the message that you are trying to deliver.	Secondly, interview others who have tried your service, product or organization to make sure that the message you delivered is exactly the message that your potential client received.	This may be the job of your customer service department or a customer response survey. You need to know before you spend years and millions on an organization that's message is not being received as you desire. If in the beginning, you ask a few strategic questions, you may solve some potentially bigger problems. For example, if I said the message of the American Red Cross is to be there for citizens that have been victims of a disaster, would you agree that that is the message that the American Red Cross is delivering? I agree. Now, they also collect blood, help on an International level as well train others to help in a disaster. I see them on the scene of disasters all over the country and around the world. So, the message of disaster relief is projected, delivered and received by all who come in contact with the team of the U. S. Red Cross.

Your message is tied to what you are saying or writing as well as to what others are saying about your organization. Additionally, your message must be produced and delivered from your organization. You can be delivering a message with your words but, not delivering that same message with your actions. The message of your organization is tied together with your words and your actions. Therefore, it should be tied to your mission. So, I ask you again as in the beginning, what is your purpose? The message that is tied to your purpose should be clear. What is your message? What is the message that you want your potential clients, customers or strategic partners to receive whether written, verbalized or published? Finally, post that purpose and message everywhere, especially in your work areas, websites, social media outlets as well as any other place that it will be viewed by potential customers.

What is your purpose?

What is Your Purpose and Message?

_____
_____
_____
_____
_____
_____
_____
_____
_____
_____
_____
_____
_____
_____
_____
_____
_____
_____
_____
_____
_____
_____
_____
_____

Products and Services

Now that you know your purpose and the message of your purpose, what are the products and services that you are going to offer that relate to your purpose and message? If you are a non-profit organization, you may be offering services without a fee because of sponsorships, donations or other funding. For our purposes, we are going to speak from the 'for-profit' vantage point.

A 'for-profit' organization is in business to make money. You should have products and services that people want, need and will buy. Just because you offer a great product or service doesn't mean that people will buy it. People will buy what they want. Lack of money doesn't even matter. People will borrow, sell something of value or take out a loan to get what they want. So, what products or services do you offer or want to offer? Products and services should take into consideration your customer, your ability to produce and your ability to deliver in a cost effective manner at the highest quality.

Also, you should have a range of products and services at prices that will meet a wide variety of budgets. For example, when you go to a large consumer store, you can find products that range from a $.99 package of gum to a $1000+ computer. There are so many products and services that a large population should be able to find something to purchase. Some stores offer food, clothes, electronics, household goods and every other product in between.

In my opinion, any person in business, ministry, or the non-profit industry should have a book. The book will grow your business. The book gives you a voice and establishes you as an expert in your industry or field of study. The book may hold the answers to questions or ease the pain of its reader. Finally, since we are discussing 'for-profit,' entities, the book is a stream of income. The book in various formats such as eBook, audio, paperback and hardback are all individual streams of income. Take that same book and translate it into a different language, a workshop, teleseminar, conference and retreat and these are all streams of income from one book. You need a book. To start, visit http://www.getstartedwithroyston.com to get on your path to being a published author.

In addition to a book, you may have other products and services that you offer. Determine if these should be categorized as signature or secondary products and services that you and your company provide. For example, a publishing company offers editing, formatting, graphic design, printing, copyrighting, distribution, coaching, training and sales of books. In addition to the physical publishing of books, there are classes, retreats, workshops and conferences associated with the publishing business. There is something for anyone who is interested in the publishing, writing, or literary industry. If you are not ready for a publishing package, there could be an online class, an introductory teleseminar or live workshop to get you started. From there you can attend workshops and retreats to help you write a book. Next, once your manuscript is ready for publishing, select one of the publishing packages that includes pricing for printing, marketing, distribution and promotional efforts. There are a lot of choices of products and services just for my company. Can you imagine the large chain retailers and the number of products and services that they have to offer?

Signature Product

What are the fundamentals and brand specific products that you will offer? If you are selling jewelry, that is the product that you sell. Let's call that your signature product. The signature product is what you sell that anyone who comes in contact with you will know that you sell. The signature product is what is on all of your promotional materials, your website, your social media outlets, and your business cards. It is what you say to people when you introduce yourself at networking events, conferences and speaking events. Just as *McDonalds* is first known for hamburgers, *Dell* is known for computer hardware, *BK Royston Publishing* is known for publishing books and *Google* is the search engine known by only one name. You, too, should have a signature product.

The signature product should always be improving, staying current and working to declare your business the number one business that sells the number one product in that industry. When considering these qualifications for a signature product, think about the products that you offer. What is your signature product? What is that product that you offer that your business is known for?

Secondary Products

Along with the Signature Product, there should be some complimentary, accessory or secondary products. The secondary products should be a natural fit with your primary products. Secondary products may come as a request or need of customers and clients, a development in the industry or an innovation of your business' creation. In my industry, book publishing is my primary product but a secondary product is coaching. Coaching writers is a natural fit because some people come to us not equipped naturally to write their story. They have a great idea for a story but need help formulating it. Coaching is something that has been a request of our customers and clients. If we didn't coach writers, then we often would not publish their books. We would be asking our clients to do something that they naturally could not do. To help grow our business and to help our clients, we offer that secondary product of coaching. What do you feel are your secondary products that you offer in your business? Over time, realize that some secondary products may become additional signature products. When you do something well, it can become something that your business is known. Keep that in mind when determining signature and secondary products.

Trial or Temporary Products

Have you ever tried out a product or service that you thought that your clients would like but they didn't accept the offering? They didn't want it; so, they didn't buy it. When people are not buying what you are selling, ask the customer, why? What's wrong with this product? Get feedback on the problems with the product, whether it be color, size, fit, delivery or quality of the product. They will tell you if you ask. In the end, make a decision. If you stick with a product that your customers are not buying, you will lose money. We established at the beginning of this chapter that this was a 'for-profit' entity and losing money is not our goal. Stop selling the product until you come up with a product that people do want to buy and make the money that you do want to make. Look at your inventory of products, what is and what isn't selling? What product do you feel that you shouldn't be offering now and may with some revision, offer again?

Seasonal Products

These are products that are available for a season or on a trial basis. In the food industry, you will see a note on the menu that says, "This is offered in season only." There are some products that are seasonal. Even with seasonal products, make sure that the product is available and that it is making you as profitable as possible. Do you provide any seasonal products to your customers?

Services

What type of services will you provide? How and when will these services be delivered? Service should be as key to a company as the product itself.

Customer Service

Customer service should be number one when it comes to your service because if people don't trust that you will take care of them, then they won't become a returning customer. People buy from who they know, like and trust. It is as simple as that. Even in the event of a mistake, error or problem with a product, if people see that you have made every good faith effort to make a correction, then they will do business with you again. In addition to them doing business with you, more importantly, they will spread the word and tell others to do business you. This has been the key to my business growth, word of mouth. I only intended for my publishing company to publish my books. Yes, I wanted to self-publish. One friend asked me to publish her book, she was satisfied and told others and they told others and so on. I am now a full-service publishing company with more than 35 authors and 80+ books published to date. This is clearly from my customer service alone. What type of customer service are you providing? If there is a problem, do you still answer your phone? If a mistake is made, do you ignore the problem or take care of it right away? If someone is happy, do you thank them promptly and offer an affiliate program of some type if your services are referred? Being nice, taking care of your customer's needs and correcting any issues that arise is an important factor in getting your message to the masses and growing your business. I guarantee that if you do not provide great service with a quality product the message will still get to the masses but it won't be a positive one. The negative reputation will proceed you and eventually, close your business.

Additional Services

Even though I run a small publishing house, I strive to perform like a major publishing house. I have the goal to be a major publishing house. At the level I am now, I need to act like I am a major publishing house. One of the things that I do that others may or may not do is provide anyone who asks about publishing with my company, a non-disclosure statement. It protects and assures you, the author, that when you discuss an idea with me that it will be kept in confidence and not disclosed.

After an author is signed with my company, there are benefits and additional services that I provide exclusively to my authors and not to others. Such as when vending, speaking or other promotional opportunities arise, I refer my authors so they can gain exposure to a larger audience when I cannot participate.

There are additional services that I provide to my customers that may not even be written or official. Some things I do because of relationship. I form a relationship with my customers throughout the publishing process. I know their heart, desires, family issues, goals and dreams. I spend the time to get to know them and not just take their money.

That's just one additional service that I provide which has led to referrals, recommendations and in truth, revenue. What services are you currently providing? What services do you need to do a better job performing? What services do you provide that are no longer profitable or necessary to the future growth of your business, non-profit or career?

Product and Service Creation

At the beginning of the chapter, we talked about the large chains of stores who offer a multiplicity of products and services at a range of prices to fit any budget. As a business owner, you have a level expertise, knowledge and experience that can be packaged. Create additional products and services which will lead to additional streams of income for your business.

For example, if your business sells shovels, you should sell the best shovels that are made at a variety of price points. There could be a small $15 shovel up to a $200 shovel which is great but, what about offering a DVD on how to best utilize that shovel? What about offering classes to help teach young people, elderly people or people with disabilities the safety side of shoveling? What about hosting a home and garden show prior to planting season that highlights all types of products that people will need for their lawns, gardens and flower beds? The DVD could be a $10 product. The safety classes could be free and then charge a company to send their people to you to teach their maintenance crew how to use a shovel properly without worker's compensation issues. The Home and Garden Show could be sponsored and other small businesses pay a fee to participate which could also generate income. With one idea, product or service, you can generate additional income. What additional products and services can you create from your existing signature, secondary and seasonal products and services?

Set a Goal

Goal setting is key to production, motivation and decision making. If you have a goal to have something completed by Friday, then there will be steps that you take to reach that goal of completion. Some people do a little bit each day on their project to make it easier to complete. Others are procrastinators and work all night on Thursday night to get it done by Friday morning. Whatever works for you is fine but having no goal is like having no aim, direction or motivation and in the end, it likely will not ever get done. Why? Because the message is not important? The purpose is not your passion and life will cause other things to take priority in your life. If you don't have a goal, life will set a goal for you. I would rather set my own goals and not let life set goals for me. I want to be the captain of my own life and not leave it in the hands of someone else.

So, what is the goal of your business, non-profit, ministry or message? You have a purpose already but what is the goal of that purpose? How will know you have arrived at your goal until you determine it, write it, work for it and achieve it? A non-written goal is not a goal.

Sales Goals

I realize that we have not talked much about sales but in general, you should have a sales goal for your products and services. It's elementary, the more you sell, the more money you make and then the more you are able to invest in producing more products. It is a production and profitability cycle. The more products and services that you have, the more customers that you will have and hopefully, these same customers will tell more customers and so on and so on.

Therefore, you need to strive for a sales goal. Based on the cost of making the product, price point that you are selling the product and the overhead to be in business, how many products or services do you need to sell to be profitable? We are in this to be profitable and not take a loss. What is the goal? What is the amount of product that you need to sell this week or this month or this year? If you sell a service and not a specific product, what is the number of appointments you have to schedule to reach your sales goals? Be sure to write the goal down. Unless the goal is written, posted or put somewhere that you will see it often, it will be easily forgotten. A posted goal will remind you and be an incentive to keep going when your rejection comes, and it will come.

Action Steps

Once you have written down the goal, what are the action steps that you are going to take to reach that goal? Write the action steps down. Put the steps on paper, post them in a place in that can't be missed and can be seen often. Next to each action step, place a projected date. You don't have to have it done perfectly by the first date you set but, you should have a projected date in mind. If not, time will continue to move and the goal may never be reached. Make sure that the goals are reasonable. If you don't know what the projected time should be to reach these goals, look it up or ask someone who has this same goal within your industry or business. Once you have the goal with your actions steps down and projected due dates, then get busy. Work on the goals each and every day. If you are serious about reaching the goals for your products and services, then there should be a designated time that you are committed to working on those goals. Even if you take thirty minutes to one hour each day to read about, work on or think about your goals, this time spent wisely will get you closer to reaching your goal. I enjoy celebrating victories in small intervals. You may not be completely finished or reached the goal entirely but, how far did you get on the first day, the first week or the first month? Stop and celebrate the small victories. Get a cup a coffee.

Call your mother and tell her the good news, anything to keep you motivated and moving.

Once the projected due date arrives, did you reach the goal? It's great if you reached it and it's great if you didn't. Why? Because if you didn't reach the goal, it gives you another opportunity to evaluate what is or is not working to reach your goal. You can also evaluate how much more time it is going to take to get there. What stopped you from reaching the goal? Finally, the goal may need to be modified from the original one. Do you need to sell five thousand of products or five hundred in order to meet your monthly budget and still be profitable? What are your products and services that you will offer? What are the goals for your products and services?

Payments and Processes

You have your purpose of your message, and the products and services are created. Now it's time to make sure that you can receive payment for what you produced. I cannot tell you how many times an author has had a book signing and they only were prepared to take cash. These same authors lost a sale because they didn't have multiple ways to accept payment. I advise authors, and business owners to not miss out on money by not having a way for people to hit the button use their credit card to pay for your products or services.

Live Events

Make sure that you have change for customers. There may or may not be a bank close by to make change for you. Other vendors or businesses don't always want to help make change so, bring your own change.

Be sure to have the device, the app and the Wi-Fi or hot spot added to your phone in order to be able to process credit cards. We live in a digital society and being able to accept credit cards is essential. Outside of the U. S. there is a charge for anything other than credit cards. Traveler's checks are a thing of the past. I have travelled abroad and some companies won't accept them because they are treated and processed just like a regular check. Even in the U. S., accepting a check is an ordeal and not a pleasant one. Be ready to accept electronic payments.

Online Payment

Your website, your social media and any other electronic communication should provide a link to make a payment or process an electronic money transfer. I say electronic money transfer because you may have to have a wire transfer from a bank instead of using PayPal or Squareup.com or other electronic payment processes. There are limits if you accept payments from out of the U. S. Some countries are not listed on PayPal's list of countries that they do business with so, I had to have a bank merchant account to transact with an overseas client. Additionally, some payment services hold large payment amounts until there is additional paperwork provided. This can happen if you do not have a track record or history of transacting business in large dollar amounts. Your ability to do business can be held up, slowed down or a customer can change their mind altogether, if you don't have a smooth and seemingly seamless way for payments to be processed.

In the end, make sure that you have established business and banking relationships with multiple outlets so as to not have your payments and essentially, your business, held up.

Processes

If a customer knows about your products, wants to buy your product and has the money to buy your product, the next thing is making it easy to not only pay for your product but have that product delivered. You should be driving people to the places where they can buy your product. If you have a standalone, brick and mortar store, you should always give the location, store hours, as well as the products and their prices. If you are doing business online, there should be a headquarters or online store for your products and services. There are many online stores and ecommerce outlets to choose from. I suggest that your online store be housed on your website, if possible or if you are using a 3rd party site, have the link to the third party from your website. This will drive traffic to your website and hopefully people will return often to your website. The point is that you need a house for your business whether it be physical or virtual. It's the same as having a house, condo or apartment for your personal items. You never want to be personally homeless and your business shouldn't be homeless either. Establish a house for your business and it shouldn't only be social media. You want to control the things that go on in your physical house. You have no control over what goes on in someone else's house and that is exactly what social media is, someone else's house.

Delivery Process

After you are paid, you need to make sure that the product or service has an easy way to be delivered. You can still have an unhappy customer if the product or service is not delivered in a safe and timely manner. In the past, pony express was used and people waited until the man on the pony arrived. Today it is not that way. Immediate comments, evaluations and reviews of your services, payments and products can be submitted via phone and other technology. Whether your products are physical or digital, people will want what they paid for to be delivered quickly and easily. Do you have an outlet for digital delivery of products, such as an .mp3 or download of an audio recording? Do you have an outlet for digital delivery of video products? Do you have a way to be notified if someone has paid for a physical product on your website so, you can mail it to them? Do you have online distribution agreement or ecommerce site with your products listed so they can be produced and delivered directly to your customers without your intervention?

Desire to have a product, plus payment for that product still requires you to have a delivery system and process to get that product to your customer. You need to have a process for delivery.

Profiles of the Team

In today's economy, people don't just like a catchy message, eye grabbing logo or even a helpful product, people want to make a connection with the people behind the message, product, service or organization. Most companies and organizations, tell the history of the company or organization and how it began. The history includes information about the leader of the organization, his or her background and how he or she began in business. People identify with the entire story of the organization and it makes them want to invest. Money is getting harder and harder to come by. There are still people out of work. There are still people that are underpaid and only able to afford the necessities of life like food, housing, basic clothing and transportation to work to get those necessities. Anything outside of the basic necessities is a luxury to some people. I reiterate to the authors of BK Royston Publishing that buying a book is a luxury to some people. If someone hands you $10 to purchase your book that should mean a lot and you should recognize that. Be nice. Be gracious. The purchase means that someone saw something in you that made them want to buy your book.

In addition to making a connection with the owner, operator, author or organization's representative, people should be able to connect with and feel your passion for the message of your organization, product or service.

Since people want to make some type of personal connection before they interact, there must be a way for people to get to know you. The most preferred method to connect with your audience is in person but, that can't always be the case. You must also be able to make connections via social media and electronic formats. A biographical introduction or sketch should be written, edited and accompanied by a good professional picture. The biographical sketch should be posted, available and updated as often as possible in a place that your potential client, strategic partner or the media will be able to access it quickly and easily.

You might ask, what should be included in a biographical sketch? I am glad you asked. A biographical sketch should contain important events and aspects about your life to date. It should always be a work in progress because you are still alive and accomplishing things every day. A biographical sketch cannot contain everything that you do every day but it should include the most important accomplishments throughout your life. As you reach milestones in your life, your biographical sketch should change.

Here are just a few of the items that should be in a biographical sketch.

- City and State of birth
- Brief synopsis of personal interests that may connect with the reader. For example, 'in his

or her spare time loves to travel, shop and make pottery.'

- Published works – books, music or art work.
- Educational Achievements
- Special Awards, and Honors

If you do not have a biographical sketch, sit down and begin to draft one. There are people who want to know more about the owner, operator or key players in your organization before they interact or conduct business with you.

Introducing yourself to your customer and even telling them something fun about you such as, I like to watch old movies, I prefer dogs over cats or I like M&Ms plain instead of with peanuts, gives people a way to make a connection with you which may in turn make a connection with your product and their credit card.

In addition to connecting with the owner or CEO of the company, introduce your team. People may not always be able to interact directly with you but may meet people on your sales team or administrative staff. Make sure that these people have your same passion, hunger and desire for the business to be great. Make sure that these are great representatives of you and your brand. They represent you so they represent your brand. Reward them when they do well. Correct them when there are issues and dismiss them if they cannot meet your standards of operation. The front line of access to you, your company and your products and services may be a long lasting positive or negative experience based on the actions of your team. What your team does is a direct reflection of what you have modeled, emphasized, tolerated and expected. Have meetings, retreats and calls that point out the behavior, attitude and character of someone associated with you and your brand. As stated earlier, the message you want to get to the masses is a positive one. Negativity always moves much faster than positivity. Give people something to be eager to associate with rather than a reason to spread negativity. These same people should have a personality of their own and shouldn't be clones of you but they should be a BEST presentation of you. They all CAN'T be you but your verbiage, values and vision should shine right through. So, who is on your team?

There are several places, ways and methods to display your biographical sketch. People need to be able to access your biographical information quickly and easily. Below is just a short list of places to make sure that your current biographical sketch is listed.

- Posted to your Organizational or Personal Website
- Profiles on Social Media Outlets
- Create and develop a Media Packet or Press Kit
- Create an electronic version of your biographical sketch to be attached to an email.

- Create a condensed or brief version of your full biography to be included on your book cover, CD covers, and social media outlets. This brief and condensed version of your full biography can also be used for media outlets with limited word count as well as an introduction at speaking engagements.

No matter where you display the biographical sketch it should be compelling, informative and inviting. Biographical sketches connect with people so that you can get your message to the masses.

Profiles of Your Team

_____

_____

_____

_____

_____

_____

_____

_____

_____

_____

_____

_____

_____

_____

_____

_____

_____

_____

_____

_____

_____

_____

_____

_____

_____

People for the Message

Up until now, we have discussed the importance of purpose, products and services, payments and process, profiles of the team, but what do you need next? You need people. There is a group of people to direct your message, products, services and purpose to. You would think that the message should be directed to everybody, anybody just whoever you can come in contact with right? No. Everybody is not going to connect with, be interested in or need the services of every organization that is out there. There are however, people who are interested in the organization and services that you have to offer. Who are they? Where do they live? What do they drive? What do they eat? How do they dress? How do they spend their money? Do they have money only at the first of the month or spend all month long? Should you be focused on men or women? Adults or children? If you don't know, ask. Put out a survey or questionnaire and ask if people would be interested in those services, products or training. Look at your message and see who really needs it. Does this message solve a problem or ease the pain of these same people? Notice where people with this particular problem gather and send your message to them as their solution. Finally, make sure your product is affordable. If people can't seem to buy your product because of the cost, you need a wider range of prices and products to appeal to a larger audience. Find a corporate sponsor who is willing to partner with you to help those who are unable to pay. It is wonderful to have a product or service but, if you don't direct it to the people who really want or need it, it will go to waste and your organization will decline, or worse, cease to exist. Who is your message directed to? Where do these people hangout, get their information and make purchases that solve their problems or satisfy their desires?

You can search high and low, use every bit of technology, chase after them in a car, tricycle or pony express but they still may or may not receive your message. I am being extreme with the use of pony express, but it caused you to pause and think about it. When you are trying to get a message across, extreme measures may have to be taken. Even with extreme measures, you still may not reach the people you intended to reach. Even with all of the forms of delivery via technology, if you are not strategic and target your intended audience, your message won't get across either. Furthermore, even being strategic, you may not obtain the support you desire. You may not attract the attention of a new client and/or sales because the message does not grab their attention or pique their interest enough to buy.

Strategy, process and consistency are keys to getting your message to the right people. It may take several interactions with your message, purpose, products or services before they buy. Don't give up. Keep going. Keep trying. Don't stop because the very time that you decide not to try, someone may buy. I like that and hope you do too.

Now, where do the people who need the message to buy your products and services hang out or get their information? Social Media analysts have determined that Pinterest members are more than 80% women. Therefore, if your message is targeted to men, Pinterest is most likely NOT the place to focus your message delivery no matter what you are posting. Social media shouldn't be your only or main method of message delivery. Remember, people still read email and may even receive snail mail. Cover all of the major outlets of message delivery. Don't ignore one area of systematic delivery because you don't think people will want your product or service. You don't know that yet. There may be someone who still likes to receive a large postcard or letter in the mail with a stamp. It's a novel idea but one that you must consider when determining who should receive and needs your message.

We talked about delivery methods earlier with products and services but think about how the people you will connect with want your message to be delivered. For example, my analytics of people who connect with me range between the ages of thirty-five to fifty-five and up. I have to have a wide range of delivery methods from digital to physical. I can't miss out on a large target market. So, if your target and acceptance audience is younger than mobile devices, digital downloads and home delivery via online ordering is what they are used to.

So, think about your audience. Should you use video with music, email, text, snail mail or phone calls? When should the message be delivered? Should the message be delivered in the morning, late evening or late night? Have you ever noticed that telemarketers call your house between the hours of 6:00 and 8:00 p.m.? Why? Because they have figured out that is when people are home and normally eating dinner. Why would they call when you are not at home and leave a message? The likelihood that you will call back, respond or act on the message is very unlikely and unprofitable. Thus, the delivery of your message must have multi-layers for effective delivery. Thinking about your audience, clientele and market and how they behave is first and foremost. Preparing an action plan of how to meet the needs and deliver your product, service or organization's message to that particular group of people must be developed so that you don't miss an opportunity to make a powerful impact.

Promotion and Marketing

Promotion and marketing involve so many things. There is word of mouth, testimonials, comments, print, digital, social media, website, billboards, business cards, television, traditional radio and internet radio that can all be used to promote and market your products, services and messages. Given your budget, all can be used simultaneously or any combination to reach your audience.

Once you have spent your money for any of the above outlets or systems to promote and market your products, services and messages as well as paying for the people involved, make sure that where ever you direct your audience is prepared, tested, easily navigated and requires as few clicks as possible. In spite of all of the social media outlets and other third party services, your message, products and services need a headquarters. The headquarters should be a website. Your website should be easily navigated and people should be able to buy your products and services within four clicks or less.

Have you ever visited a visually striking and beautifully created website but couldn't navigate your way through the website very well? The website was appealing to the eye. The colors were bright and cheerful. The pictures were enticing and made you ready to make a purchase but, you couldn't find the button to click to make that purchase happen. The ability for people to easily and quickly respond to a message is just as important as the message itself. If people don't have the ability to respond to the message easily and quickly, then you might as well not deliver it at all. The results of the delivery of the message will be the same, nothing. Investment in marketing strategies and social media outlets is wonderful but, the intended audience should be able to buy, respond with a comment, upload a document or get a receipt for their purchase in three clicks or less.

The website or social media page should clearly mark the button that you intend for people to respond to. 'Click on the item you want to buy', 'donation' or 'send an email for more information' should stand out in a bold picture that has working hyperlinks to the next steps. If the link is plain text, the text should stand out in bold, enlarged font apart from the regular body of the advertisement so, it can be quickly distinguished from all other text. The links should be tested by the creator, developer and those outside of your server access to make sure that they work. You don't want to miss any opportunities once your site, account, email or e-blast goes live. The necessary steps need to be determined and limited for your audience or client to respond to your message. For example, to purchase my books, you can visit my website, www.bkroystonpublishing.com, go to the store and click on the book, purchase it through PayPal and press submit. This should take three clicks. Type in a few pieces of information for delivery and payment and then the book is on the way to you. If you search for my materials on Amazon, you can pay in one click with a credit card on file. Eliminate the delay in responding to your message as much as possible. There should not be more than two webpages that a person should have to click on to respond to your message. In our scan, select and delete society, people lose interest VERY quickly and will not respond to your message as intended thus, missing out on a sale or connection. Promotion and marketing take money, time and effort in order to attract, drive and engage people enough to buy. Don't make it harder for them to buy once they go to your website. It should be as easy as possible.

In addition to your website, make sure that you have picked brand colors that are attractive to your audience. If you don't know what your audience likes, ask them before you invest in branding colors and marketing and promotional tools. Once you know what your client or audience is attracted to, make sure that your logo is in those colors and the image represents exactly what you are selling. Make sure that it's not vague or confusing. My logo is in the shape of book. That's what I do, publish books. It's not confusing. It is straight forward and to the point. Remember that you are not trying to make this business of getting your message to the masses hard but as easy and as clear as possible.

Invest in a professional photographer for your photos. This is a great investment and will pay off in the long run. You just need a few shots that represent you and your brand. Photoshoots are suggested so that you have the proper lighting, poses with make-up and wardrobe that best suit you and attract people to you rather than repel people. People are extremely visual. It does make a difference how you look. People will decide to do business with you based on how you look. If you don't care how you look, your customer or audience may think that if they hire you, you may not care about their money, project or idea and decide not to do business with you. People may never get to your talent, gifts and abilities based on the visual image that you are projecting. It does matter so, get professional photos done and dress professionally at the event that you attend.

The biggest promotional tool and outlet is you. People do business with people that they are attracted to, trust and like. So many times, I have had people say, "I like your spirit." If that helps people feel comfortable enough to do business with me, then so be it. Let's sign a contract. Sure, I had my website in order, my business cards were ready, I was dressed for the event and I had a bright smile on my face but it was still once people met me, they wanted to do business with me.

Platform

Every time you speak about your business, promote your business, conduct your business, you are building a platform and wider audience to be attracted and connect with your business. Therefore, the more you talk about it, the further reach you have and the higher you are building the platform. A platform is a stand, position or representation of a specific industry or issue that you, your business or organization and message has taken upon itself. I have built a platform of informative, entertaining and insightful books in all formats. When people meet me or have done business with me, they know I publish books. Every year that my business has been in existence, every client that has been satisfied and recommends me and every time a new client comes to me based on that recommendation, that is another brick, stone or floor built onto my platform. I just keep going higher and higher, wider and wider.

Because of my publishing platform, I am now asked to speak about my books, publishing other people's books, promotion of books as well as creating other products and services based on an author's book. With creating other products and services, I am continuing to build my content creation and message delivery platform. I not only help people publish books but plan conferences, workshops, retreats, programs, reports, lead magnets and eBooks for their content. People want to experience content in different formats than just a paperback book. The old song says, "Give the people what they want." I now realize that I have to help authors create multiple outlets for their message which produce multiple streams of income.

The message may stay the same but, the methods of delivering that message can change. Over the years, we have seen people's platforms rise to global success through only one book to one audience. One of my favorite examples of this is Bishop T. D.

Jakes. He turned a Sunday school class with one book and a handful of people into a multi-million dollar platform complete with books, movies, a television show, mega church, conferences, workshops, retreats and a household name. He spoke continually two words, "get ready" repeatedly three times in row. Why? It doesn't matter why but it worked. That was his slogan, he is a dynamic speaker and teacher, he is an administrative and creative genius, gifted and anointed beyond words. Presidents, heads of state, heads of corporations, organizations and ministries around the world seek his council and they have been the bricks, stone, mortar and beams that have built his platform to speak to nations.

I realize that Bishop Jakes was appointed, called, has the experience and connections to command the audience to come from around the world to participate in his platform. Now, he is "The Bishop Jakes." He wasn't always "The Bishop Jakes" that we know now. He had to start somewhere and you do too.

I take from him three things, preparation, consistency and evolution. When you hear him speak, he is prepared; his slogan, products and message were consistent for many years until everyone knew it. He continues to evolve and change with the times in which we live to meet the needs of the people he wants to reach.

Think about your own message and who you want to benefit from that message. The first few times he said, "Get ready" three times in a row, I know that some people laughed and made fun of him saying it. Why? People don't applaud innovation right away because most people fear change. If people don't understand something, they make fun of it first and then applaud it later when it is a household phrase and has made millions. Who is laughing at him now? No one. The world now knows that that is his phrase and whether it is patented, trademarked or not, anyone else who would try to build a platform on it would fail especially in the church because it would be a clear copy.

What message, phrase, slogan, hashtag, product or service are you consistently delivering? It may take years for the message to build a platform for all of the world to see, but know that someone is looking. Someone is watching at all times. They see your platform even if you don't. They see how tall your platform is getting, how many people are attracted to you, how many new clients you have, what you post on social media even if they never like or share it. Your platform may be taller than you even know. Pause and look around you. Who knows you that you may not even know? Your email list may deceive you as well. There are more people that know that haven't even signed up to be on your mailing list.

One final thing, be careful who you connect your platform with. I had a friend whose house caught on fire because of a short in wiring. It was no neglect or accident on her or her family's it just happened. Unfortunately, the fire spread and because the houses were so close, two other houses caught on fire. My point is that if you are standing and building your platform close to and/or partnering with someone who doesn't do business like you and doesn't handle their message carefully and with integrity like you, you could catch on fire and be destroyed by standing and linking up too close. Protect your platform. What took years to build could only take a matter of seconds and a few clicks on the computer to destroy.

Partnerships and Collaboration

When getting your message to the masses you need as many references, helpers, word of mouth advertisers and references for using your business as possible. With all of the technology that is available, recommendations and word of mouth are still the best promotional tool for your message. Technology will never be eliminated as a means of delivering your message. Technology will be used by Social Media outlets such as Facebook, Twitter or Pinterest to locate, share, like and promote someone else's product, service, website or social media pages.

Remember that we live in a global society and are not limited to a specific city, region or continent. Today, we have the power to recommend, refer, partner and collaborate with people anywhere in the world. We never have to meet the person physically to do business or partner with them. You can find out a person's business, products and services, get referrals, sign contracts, make money exchanges and do business with them and not shake their physical hand. There are unlimited possibilities and monumental implications for partnership and other connections with like companies and persons around the global with the use of technology.

For partnerships and collaborations to be successful, there are some things to consider:

Do you even want to partner or collaborate with someone else? You have to ask yourself can you work with someone else. This may seem like a dumb question but it is true. Some people want the benefits of partnership but don't know how to conduct themselves in a partnership. You have to detail out the roles and responsibilities of each person involved. Will we email, fax or mail agreements? How will products and services be determined? There should be a contract signed by each party agreeing to the duties, terms, risks, liabilities, length of the agreement and a way to dissolve the partnership and/or and collaboration. International businesses have different customs, legalities, rules and regulatory guidelines for doing business that cannot be assumed to apply or be adhered to if you live in the United States. If necessary, you may have to obtain the services of an International attorney to know the protocol and especially the liability if something happens to go wrong with an International partnership.

Your first partners and obligation should be to the people who have actually utilized your services, product or had business dealings with your organization. These people who have experienced you, your products and services and have contributed to your growth, marketing and existence as a business, organization, non-profit or ministry. When they paid you money to buy any of your products or services whether it is a $10 book, $500 class or $2000 retreat or conference, they are your partner. You owe them something. You may not be a public company that pays dividends quarterly or annually but these partners believe in you, invested and they should get a return on their investment. What should be returned to them? You should continue doing business in excellence. You should maintain the highest quality control, customer service and integrity when handling your business. Amongst these partners, there may be another business venture that you can participate in. So, keep moving forward doing the right thing and you never know how working with this first group of partners will be mutually beneficial. When people have a good experience, you will have their support, repeat patronage and free advertisement to others about their satisfaction. Don't let your first partners down.

Secondly, develop strategic partnerships. What is a strategic partner? A strategic partner is someone that you develop a partnership with that is inside the norm and clearly a mutually beneficial partnership. You also may have some of the same customers or audiences that you are trying to gain the attention of and if you work together you should be able to get twice as much done with less effort. For example, if you are a company that makes freezers and you find a partner who makes frozen products, this should be a win/win. Each partner's customers could possibly want the frozen products and if purchased, will need the freezer. It is possible, to promote your products simultaneously, the frozen foods or products and the freezers to keep them frozen. This is a strategic partnership that should be profitable to each company. The negatives of this process are if both companies are not recommending the other company. You can't make people buy the frozen foods/products or the freezer but it is much more convenient to have both organizations available for purchase quickly and easily. With this partnership, the customer should be satisfied with the freezer and the products that go into the freezer in order to make the process a win/win for all involved.

Third example, there are companies that you can partner with that may not need your product or service but, wish to develop an entire package of different companies to service or sponsor a larger company or event. For example, a large outdoor event will need multiple companies to help make the event a success. There have been event planners who assemble a team of multiple companies to satisfy a variety of needs. Food vendors, security, entertainment, contractors who assemble exhibitor booths, non-profit organizations that need to get their message to the general public masses. All of these industry examples mentioned may not normally partner but, can and would love to partner on a larger scale to a major event or organization for the marketing, promotion and exposure to a different audience who may not normally come in contact with their business. The partnership may be temporary or long-term depending on the results of the event. Because you are participating in an event with other companies or organizations, you are sharing expenses and more likely to get media exposure which gets your message to an even wider audience that may or may not have attended the event.

Finally, think outside of the box when developing relationships for partnerships. This may require that you get out of your comfort zone, your city, state or even country. Networking and partnering with a diverse group of companies can diversify your audience and potentially gain new customers for you.

A word of caution, get references, recommendations, ask people don't just take someone's word for what they can do and bring to the table. Follow people online. Read comments. Reach out to people that you see are connected with these companies, people and organizations that you think that may make a good partnership or collaboration. LinkedIN.com provides places for people to actually give recommendations to people. Don't ignore the recommendations, follow-up. Even after you have a strong recommendation, make sure that you have a signed agreement, in some cases, especially if you are paying money or offering your products or services in exchange for these partnerships. Sit down, talk, webinar, videoconference with these people before entering into a partnership. Also, try to partner with companies that have your same work ethic, mindset toward business and moral code for business and partnering. Mistakes will be made and trusting people is always a journey but if it turns out to be a mistake, then so be it. Learn from the mistake, correct it and move forward with a better understanding of what you need and expect in a partnership.

Think outside of the box, diversity is a wonderful way to gain new clients, be bold, a maverick and take calculated risks but, don't potentially ruin your business' reputation, clientele and product or services by doing business with people who have a disreputable or unethical reputation.

Who Have You Partnered With or Desire to Partner With?

_____

_____

_____

_____

_____

_____

_____

_____

_____

_____

_____

_____

_____

_____

_____

_____

_____

_____

_____

_____

_____

_____

Pause to Grow

A business that is not changing, evolving, improving or being evaluated will soon die. Now that you are getting your message out to the masses how will improve your organization, business, product or service?

In the education business, teachers, administrators and parents are always looking and comparing data of the individual student with the national benchmarks of other students to determine how their individual student is progressing toward their learning goals. In business you must do the same. How did your last sales campaign turn out? Did you have the sales volume that you anticipated? What do your customers say about your products and services? What is your engagement on social media, your website or in a live event or brick or mortar store? Who does your message, or products and services appeal to? Men, women, young people? Members of the United States, Europe,

Asia, Africa? Do your customers respond to emails, radio, television, newspapers, magazine ads and/or social media referrals? You must know the answer to these and many more questions. Why? The answers will determine the direction of your business, the ability for your business to remain in existence, how your message should change, how your products and services should change and maybe the overall structure and purpose of business should change. Pause to Grow.

There are times that you are so busy working, producing and creating the products, services and the new messages that you want to get out that you haven't paused to ask your audience what they want or reviewed what they said they wanted before moving forward with the next campaign. Pause, Reflect, Evaluate, Tweak and Relaunch to Grow.

The numbers don't lie. The comments don't lie. The evaluations don't lie. The hard cold facts will let you know how to improve the delivery, reception and response to your message. You are in business to profit. You are in business to grow. You are not in business to fail. When something doesn't work, ask. When something doesn't sell, ask. When you are broke, find the people that are succeeding and rich in your industry. Follow them on social media to find out how and what they do. Don't re-create the wheel. Look at what someone else is doing and modify it to fit your company, budget and product needs.

Business is cyclical and there are cycles or phases in business. There is the creation phase, research and development phase, the implementation phase and then finally the evaluation phase and then you start the process all over again. In the creation phase, you are creating the product, service or organization.

In each phase, there should be some documentation or data related to it. Before you start creating anything, is there a need for what you are offering?

Do people even want what you are thinking about creating? Ask a question and see how people respond online. People love to offer their opinions online especially on social media whether you want them or not.

Don't spend money creating something that people don't want or need. Before I publish a book, I put the cover out there. I often have two versions of a book cover. I ask which one they like. Based on the book cover alone, I get people who want to know what the book is about, and when it will be available. I pause long enough to do some research, homework, ask some questions, and then release the book because of these things, I should be more successful with my book sales. I recently did a romance fiction series and posted versions of the book cover and let people vote. The engagement from friends and followers was incredible. There were people from all over the world that put their comments under the pictures.

There are times that you are brainstorming about producing something new, determine what is already out in the market place. Ask yourself if you are creating something unique or offering a repeat of what is already out there? Strive to be unique, different and stand out from the crowd. There is a movement to start businesses, increase your business and even leave the job to start a business. It is competitive out there. What do you do that attracts people to you rather than repels them? What have your customers said that they like most about working with you? Do more of that! Tell more people about that. Offer an affiliate fee or special promotion for people who tell others about what you do. Watch your business take off and grow. It will surprise you.

In the preparation phase, review your inventory, examine your current resources, make a needs assessment and connect with others to make sure you are ready for the next phase of implementation.

Determine a timeline for implementation at three months, six months and one year prior to roll out or implementation of your product or service.

Once you are prepared, take action and go to the next phase of implementation. The implementation phase is where you put into action what you have created and prepared all of your entities from sales, marketing, promotion and production to be ready to get the product and/or service to your customers. Once you have taken your product, service or business and exposed it to the physical or virtual world, what's next? You are back in the evaluation phase again. Did it work? Did it hit or miss? Did people buy, sign-up or inquire about it or just ignore it and scroll past it like everything else? These are only a few of the things you should consider in the evaluation phase. You are not done. Once you are in the evaluation phase unless you reached all of your goals, sold out of all of your product or crashed your phone or computer server with orders, you need to go back through the phases again. This time you are making adjustments, tweaking and refining your message based on your responses in the evaluation phase and any other follow-up evaluations and interviews from actual clients or customers.

Remember your message is vital to society, don't let your delivery method or initial responses to your message stop you. Refine it, change it and re-deliver the message again and again until you receive the results that you desire or start from scratch.

Reflection, Retreats and Re-visits

In the last quarter of the year, there is a lot of time spent on sales, marketing and promotion of products and services during the biggest selling time of year. In the midst of all of that selling, working and pushing, take some time one day, one weekend to reflect, retreat and re-visit the past nine months or year. In business, there is never a time to stop but you must pause. You must think about what all you did the past year. Reflect on how you felt during certain times of the year. How did you handle the situation? What could you have done better or differently? What things were out of your control? What decisions did you make that you are happy about or others that you regret? You must review this or you repeat it in the upcoming New Year or business cycle. If it is something that didn't turn out, you have to review even more. Why? Because multiple failures or not so good business decisions will be too much for you emotionally and physically and spill over into your business affairs and your business will be crushed or destroyed from the weight.

About the Author

Julia Royston is an author, publisher, speaker, teacher and songwriter residing in Southern Indiana with her husband, Brian K. Royston. To her credit, Julia has written original music for five CDs, two DVDs, authored twenty-eight Books, and served as a contributing author for three books. Julia and her husband spend their spare time overseeing the operations of three companies and a non-profit organization. BK Royston Publishing, LLC and Royal Media Publishing to provide quality, informative, inspirational and entertaining materials in the global market place in all media formats. Julia Royston Enterprises is a writing and business consulting firm to assist aspiring authors and business owners get their message to the masses. For the Kingdom Ministries is a non-profit organization that is established to encourage, enlighten and empower people to live the abundant life and walk in purpose and destiny. Julia is a retired certified, technology teacher and librarian. For more information visit www.bkroystonpublishing.com, www.royalmediaandpublishing.com,

or www.juliaroyston.net.

To purchase her books, visit
http://www.roystonroyalbookstore.com.

Follow Julia on Social Media
Facebook, Twitter, LinkedIn, Instagram, YouTube
and TikTok.

www.ingramcontent.com/pod-product-compliance
Lightning Source LLC
Chambersburg PA
CBHW071116210326
41519CB00020B/6313